Nora Perry

After the Ball

And Other Poems

Nora Perry

After the Ball
And Other Poems

ISBN/EAN: 9783744652728

Printed in Europe, USA, Canada, Australia, Japan

Cover: Foto ©Thomas Meinert / pixelio.de

More available books at **www.hansebooks.com**

AFTER THE BALL,

AND OTHER POEMS.

BY

NORA PERRY.

BOSTON:
JAMES R. OSGOOD AND COMPANY,
LATE TICKNOR & FIELDS, AND FIELDS, OSGOOD, & CO.
1875.

Entered according to Act of Congress, in the year 1874,
BY JAMES R. OSGOOD & CO.,
in the Office of the Librarian of Congress, at Washington.

UNIVERSITY PRESS : WELCH, BIGELOW, & CO.,
CAMBRIDGE.

TO MY MOTHER.

CONTENTS.

	PAGE
AFTER THE BALL	9
THE LAST RIDE	15
THE ROMANCE OF A ROSE	21
COINCIDENCE	28
ARMIDA	38
NORTH AND SOUTH	44
MAGDALENA	52
AN AUTUMN BOUQUET	59
THE BLACK SHAWL	62
JANE	68
PEPITA	74
THE GARDEN OF THE LILIES	78
IN AN HOUR	85
UPHARSIN	88
YESTERNIGHT	92
AN ACQUAINTANCE	96
HER SECRET	98
JENNY	101
TWO VIEWS	103
HAUNTED	106
HESTER BROWNE	108

CONTENTS.

Destiny	110
Loss and Gain	113
Homeless	115
La Sirène	117
Tying her Bonnet under her Chin	119
That Waltz of Von Weber's	122
Half an Hour	127
Polly	133
Bess and Ben	138
Blanche's Châteaux	143
Apple-Blossoms	148
In June	152
Another Year	155
Some Day of Days	158
Cecily	160
Riding Down	165
Somebody's Humming-Bird	169
Sylvia's Song	176
Thorns	178
"And a little Child shall lead them"	180
What may be	182
Circe	184
My Lady	186
And now I sit down daily with a face	188
Misunderstood	189
Out of the Window	191

AFTER THE BALL,

AND OTHER POEMS.

AFTER THE BALL.

THEY sat and combed their beautiful hair,
　Their long bright tresses, one by one,
As they laughed and talked in the chamber there,
　　After the revel was done.

Idly they talked of waltz and quadrille;
　Idly they laughed, like other girls,
Who over the fire, when all is still,
　　Comb out their braids and curls.

Robes of satin and Brussels lace,
　Knots of flowers and ribbons too,

Scattered about in every place,
    For the revel is through.

And Maud and Madge in robes of white,
    The prettiest nightgowns under the sun,
Stockingless, slipperless, sit in the night,
    For the revel is done.

Sit and comb their beautiful hair,
    Those wonderful waves of brown and gold,
Till the fire is out in the chamber there,
    And the little bare feet are cold.

Then out of the gathering winter chill,
    All out of the bitter St. Agnes weather,

While the fire is out and the house is still,
    Maud and Madge together, —

Maud and Madge in robes of white,
    The prettiest nightgowns under the sun,
Curtained away from the chilly night,
    After the revel is done, —

Float along in a splendid dream,
    To a golden gittern's tinkling tune,
While a thousand lustres shimmering stream,
    In a palace's grand saloon.

Flashing of jewels and flutter of laces,
    Tropical odors sweeter than musk,

Men and women with beautiful faces
    And eyes of tropical dusk, —

And one face shining out like a star,
    One face haunting the dreams of each,
And one voice sweeter than others are,
    Breaking into silvery speech, —

Telling, through lips of bearded bloom,
    An old, old story over again,
As down the royal bannered room,
    To the golden gittern's strain,

Two and two, they dreamily walk,
    While an unseen spirit walks beside,

And, all unheard in the lovers' talk,
    He claimeth one for a bride.

O Maud and Madge, dream on together,
    With never a pang of jealous fear!
For, ere the bitter St. Agnes weather
    Shall whiten another year,

Robed for the bridal, and robed for the tomb,
    Braided brown hair and golden tress,
There'll be only one of you left for the bloom
    Of the bearded lips to press, —

Only one for the bridal pearls,
    The robe of satin and Brussels lace,

Only one to blush through her curls
    At the sight of a lover's face.

O beautiful Madge, in your bridal white,
    For you the revel has just begun ;
But for her who sleeps in your arms to-night
    The revel of life is done ! .

But, robed and crowned with your saintly bliss,
    Queen of heaven and bride of the sun,
O beautiful Maud, you'll never miss
    The kisses another hath won !

THE LAST RIDE.

THERE was red wine flowing from the flagons,
The jewel-crusted flagons slim and tall,
And a hundred voices, laughing, jesting,
And a hundred toasts ringing down the hall;
For the baron held a feast at the castle,
The gay young baron, lithe and tall.

From the daïs-steps the red drums beating,
And the horns and the silver trumpets blowing,
And the quick sweet rasping of the fiddles,
Set the dancers in the dance-room a-going;

And all through the palace ran the music,
And all night the red wine was flowing.

And the baron led the wassail and the dance,
The gay young baron, lithe and tall,
With gallant smiles and jests for the lovely women guests,
Till the cock crew athwart the castle wall;
But amid the lovely faces rising out of ruffs and laces,
One face for the baron shone fairer than them all.

He had stolen from the drinking and the dancing,
He was standing in the doorway at her side;
He was praying, he was pleading and entreating,

A suit she coquetted and denied
He was praying, he was pleading and entreating,
When the blast of a bugle far and wide

Rang its clear silver treble in the court-yard,
Three times three, for a sharp battle-call;
And the voice of a trooper hoarsely shouted,
"Ho, barons, for the king, one and all!"
Round and round, over hill and over valley,
Far and wide rang the sharp battle-call.

Round and round rang the news of the rising,
The rising of old Coventry that night;
And the barons, one and all, at the bugle's bat-
    tle-call,
Mustered forth, fifty strong, for the fight.

Corslets ringing, feathers flinging, pennons swinging, —
O, it must hăve been a spirit-stirring sight!

Women's faces grew as white as the rose, —
The white rose of York upon each breast;
Red lips in that moment lost their blooming,
Gay hearts in that moment lost their jest.
But out of fifty faces, sorrow-saddened,
There was one face sadder than the rest.

Eyes that a moment since disdained him,
Lips that were laughing and denying,
Heart that coquetted with its wooing,
Now on the wooer's breast is lying;

While the bugle rings its blast, and the troopers rattle past,
Over hill and over valley flying, flying.

And the baron rides last, but the baron rides fast,
Over hill and over valley, rides away ;
With a smile upon his face, and with a gallant grace,
As if he rode to tournament, or a hunting holiday.
But in the early dawning, in the gray of the morning,
In the front of the fight, his white plumes play.

And in the early dawning, in the gray of the morning,
The red field is won ere the day's half begun ;

And the cavaliers are shouting, at the round-
    heads routing,
Till over hill and valley comes creeping up the sun;
Then the shouts and the cheers turn suddenly
    to tears,
For there on the field, his brief race run,

White and still in the dawning of the wild
    autumn morning,
White and still, in the chill of the new-risen day,
While the roundheads are flying, the hero lies
    dying,
Who so late rode straight in the front of the fray;
With a smile upon his face, and with a gallant
    grace,
As if he rode to tournament or a hunting holiday.

THE ROMANCE OF A ROSE.

IT is nearly a hundred years ago
Since the day the Count de Rochambeau —
Our ally against the British crown —
Met Washington in Newport town.

'T was the month of March, and the air was chill,
But, bareheaded, over Aquidneck hill,
Guest and host they took their way,
While on either side in grand display

A gallant army, French and fine,
Was ranged three deep in a glittering line;

And the French fleet sent a welcome roar
Of a hundred guns from Conanicut shore;

And the bells rang out from every steeple,
And from street to street the Newport people
Followed and cheered, with a hearty zest,
De Rochambeau and his honored guest

And women out of the windows leant,
And out of the windows smiled and sent
Many a coy admiring glance
To the fine young officers of France.

And the story goes that the belle of the town
Kissed a rose and flung it down

Straight at the feet of De Rochambeau ;
And the gallant Marshal, bending low,

Lifted it up with a Frenchman's grace,
And kissed it back with a glance at the face
Of the daring maiden where she stood,
Blushing out of her silken hood.

That night at the ball, still the story goes,
The Marshal of France wore a faded rose
In his gold-laced coat, but he looked in vain
For the giver's beautiful face again.

Night after night, and day after day,
The Frenchman eagerly sought, they say,

At feast or at church or along the street,
For the girl who flung her rose at his feet.

And she, night after night, day after day,
Was speeding farther and farther away
From the fatal window, the fatal street,
Where her passionate heart had suddenly beat

A throb too much, for the cool control
A Puritan teaches to heart and soul;
A throb too much for the wrathful eyes
Of one who had watched in dismayed surprise

From the street below: and taking the gauge
Of a woman's heart in that moment's rage,

He swore, this old colonial squire,
That before the daylight should expire,

This daughter of his, with her wit and grace,
Her dangerous heart, and her beautiful face,
Should be on her way to a sure retreat,
Where no rose of hers could fall at the feet

Of a curséd Frenchman, high or low:
And so while the Count De Rochambeau,
In his gold-laced coat, wore a faded flower,
And awaited the giver hour by hour,

She was sailing away in the wild March night
On the little deck of the sloop "Delight";

Guarded even in the darkness there
By the wrathful eyes of a jealous care.

Three weeks after, a brig bore down
Into the harbor of Newport town,
Towing a wreck, — 't was the sloop "Delight":
Off Hampton rocks, in the very sight

Of the land she sought, she and her crew,
And all on board of her, full in view
Of the storm-bound fishermen over the bay,
Went to their doom on that April day.

When Rochambeau heard the terrible tale,
He muttered a prayer, for a moment grew pale,

Then, "*Mon Dieu!*" he exclaimed, "so my fine
    romance,
From beginning to end, is a rose and a glance!"

A rose and a glance, with a kiss thrown in;
That was all, — but enough for a promise of sin,
Thought the stern old squire, when he took the
    gauge
Of a woman's heart in that moment's rage.

So the sad old story comes to a close:
'T is a century since, but the world still goes
On the same base round, still takes the gauge
Of its highest hearts in a moment's rage.

COINCIDENCE.

A PRETTY place it is to see,
Rose-hedged, and fairly held in fee
By larches and the linden-tree.

The roses fall, the daisies droop,
And all about the ancient stoop
The eager sparrows soar and swoop.

We hear the robins chirp and call,
We see the almond-blossoms fall,
The peaches 'neath the garden wall.

But not a human voice is heard

To break the voice of bee or bird,

And not a human hand has stirred

The almond-blossoms, as they fall,

The peaches 'neath the garden wall,

For years around this ancient " Hall."

The hand that latest plucked the rose,

Or broke the blushing almond-blows,

Or stirred the fruit from its repose,

The feet that latest pressed the ground,

The voice that latest echoed round,

Is in what sleep enchanted bound?

Upon a far-off foreign street,
Where only foreign voices greet,
Are wandering the alien feet.

And foreign fruits and foreign flowers
Are plucked within their Southern bowers
By English hands in summer hours.

The voice that once sang prayer and praise
In English chapels, now doth raise,
In Tuscan gardens, Tuscan lays.

But wearily the footsteps fall,
And palace pleasures sadly pall
Upon the alien from the " Hall."

In Tuscan gardens far away

She hears the lark's delightful lay,

She sees the sparrows dart and play.

In Tuscan palaces she hears

A voice from out the distant years,

That floods her heart in sudden tears.

In Tuscan twilights she doth miss,

Amid her royalty, the kiss

That once thrilled all her soul with bliss.

She'll never lose that fond caress,

Although another's lip may press

The cheek, the mouth, the golden tress.

O Love that was so sorely tried,
Yet parted in an hour of pride, —
Where shall the bridegroom find his bride?

Ah! ne'er on any lover's breast
Will that proud head find utter rest,
Or go she east or go she west.

None knoweth this so well as she
Who wanders there beyond the sea,
Searching in vain the golden key

Which openeth the golden gate,
The portal of a visioned Fate
Where Consolation sits in state.

COINCIDENCE.

What consolation doth she seek,

With such a burning, fevered cheek,

And haughty brows that shame the meek?

Within ambition's lofty gains

She strives to dull Love's tender pains;

All other comfort she disdains.

The laurel crown is forming fast,

She feels its royal weight at last,

And thinks the triumph slays the past.

O woman heart, ye'll find again

The burning fire, the tender pain,

For Love will never thus be slain!

The hour approached, — the moment came!

An idle guest pronounced a name, —

And flashed anew the sentient flame;

Flashed through and through her haughty calm,

And scorched the laurel's potent charm,

Dispelled for aye its transient balm.

"O Love!" she cries, "return to me!

I'd barter all the world for thee!

O, once again to hear, to see,

"To feel that tenderest embrace,

His breath across my happy face,

My head to find the resting-place

"It found in those delightful hours
When Love was crowned with fairer flowers
Than ever bloomed in Tuscan bowers!"

Was Love so mighty? Could it be
Through miles of space across the sea,
This tender cry, this passion-plea,

Was heard by him on English ground,
As one may hear a sudden sound,
And stand in wondering silence bound?

For thus above the rise and fall
Of music in a festive hall,
He heard a wild, impassioned call.

And in a strange bewildering trance
He lost the gay saloon, the dance,
He lost the countess' tender glance,

And stood within a garden shade,
Where larches and the linden made
A well-remembered garden glade.

It was the hour, the very same,
When in her Tuscan home there came
A sudden presence fine as flame.

"My Love," she cries, "he comes for me!
My Love, my Love, he waits for me!"
Then turned her face towards the sea, —

COINCIDENCE. 37

Her face with awe and rapture blent,

And slowly, slowly, downward bent

Her weary head, as if she leant

Against some tender sheltering breast.

So ended all her weary quest,

So entered she upon her rest.

And while from Tuscany there sped

To England's shores the tidings dread,

That she, the laurel-crowned, was dead,

Friends, clustering round an English tomb,

Spoke softly, awe-struck in the gloom,

Of this coincidence of doom.

ARMIDA.

I TO be brought at her feet
As a falcon brings a bird;
I to be troubled or stirred,
Whenever I chance to meet

A face that happens to grow
The lily and rose, on a skin
Satin-textured and thin, —
I to be brought so low!

I to care whether her eyes
Seek another, or shine

As I look, back to mine,
Telling their laughing love-lies !

Or if her hand touches *my* hand,
Ringless, and gloveless, and fair,
As smiling she passes me there,
Where grimly unsmiling I stand !

Last night, in dancing, she grazed
My foot with the hem of her gown,
And there I stood looking down
At the silk as if I were dazed.

And when, with that hand's white wonder,
She lifted the shawl

Which had hindered my fall,
How I inwardly cursed my blunder!

And I cursed *her* under my breath,
  As she smiled on me there,
  For I knew, false and fair,
She would lead men on to the death

That lurks in a woman's art;
  Worst of all a woman like this,
  With her smile like another's kiss,
And her cold unoccupied heart.

All the time I was cursing her there
  Her hand was over my arm,

And her face shining calm
Out of its brown chestnut hair;

Shining serenely and still,
  As we paced down the room,
  And entered the gloom
Of the garden, led by her will.

Poor fool! I remember e'en yet
  How the heliotrope scent
  Wafted up as we went,
And the smell of the crushed mignonette,

As through the dim alleys we strolled
  In the night soft and still,

Until suddenly over the hill
Lightning flashed and low thunder rolled.

What madness then clouded my brain?
  For I kissed her fears into rest,
  As she clung to my breast
In the tumult of wind and of rain.

'T was the madness of folly and wine;
  For what did I care,
  Though I knew she was fair,
When I knew she could never be mine?

Mine! though she knelt to me here
  With that hand for a gift,

Not a hand would I lift
To gather it ever so near.

I shall never be fooled like the rest,
So do not class me with those
Who would kneel for the rose
She wears on her beautiful breast;

Nor speak to me now of her power:
I tell you 't was wine,
Youth's folly and wine,
That made me her slave in that hour!

NORTH AND SOUTH.

FORT ADAMS.

I. — 1860.

SHE leaped up, laughing, all alone
Upon the rampart's sodden stone,

And, laughing, hid behind the mouth
Of the great cannon, facing south.

"Ah! will he find me here?" she said,
Then hushed her laugh and shook her head.

"Nay, will he miss me from the rest,
And, missing, care to come in quest?"

But dancing eyes deride the doubt,
The deprecating lips breathe out,

And waiting, waiting all alone,
Upon the rampart's sodden stone,

She looks across the cannon's mouth,
The silent cannon facing south;

Across the great ships riding down
In stately silence to the town;

Across the sea just where the mist
Melts all the blue to amethyst,

From whence the wind o'er all the sails
Blew soft that day its southern gales.

But white-sailed ships that rode the sea,
Nor dusky cannon's mouth saw she,

With those young eyes whose wistful gaze
Went dreaming thwart the purple- haze ;

Instead, beyond the white-sailed ships,
Beyond the cannon's dusky lips,

Beyond the sea just where the mist
Melts all the blue to amethyst,

The tall palmettoes darkly rise
Before her dream-enchanted eyes,

And waiting, waiting all alone
Upon the rampart's sodden stone,

In dreams she stands beneath the shade
Of Southern palms, — this little maid,

Whose morning face and tender eyes
Took all their hue from Northern skies.

And standing thus enchanted there,
Within her castle of the air,

The rippling tide, that sinks and swells,
Comes to her ear like wedding bells;

And through her castle's airy halls,
From room to room a low voice calls,

And calling, calling, near, so near,
That half in dream and half in fear

She turns, and swift her vision flies
Before the vision of her eyes;

For some one scales the rampart mound,
And some one laughs: "Ah, truant, found!"

And face to face she meets him there,
Her fairy castle's lordly heir!

So, North and South, the pine and palm,
United, in that summer calm

Of idle summer days they stand,
By prosperous gales and breezes fanned.

II.— 1862.

No summer guests with curious gaze
Stroll now beneath the "covered ways,"

And gayly laugh and speculate
Upon the old Fort's useless state.

Where last year's lonely arches rang
With idle voices, girls who sang

Their airy songs, or sent their call
From sodden stone or rampart wall,

There echoes now the martial tread
Of soldier sentinels instead.

And they who, sailing through the mist,
Came hither for a lover's tryst,

And vowed next year again to stand
Thus face to face, thus hand to hand,

Upon the old Fort's mouldering mound, —
Where find they now a trysting ground?

Upon Manassas' bloody plain
One keeps a tryst with death and pain;

And one, grown old before her years
Of youth have fled, with anguished tears

Wrung from despair, far out of reach
Of love's last touch, of love's last speech,

By Narragansett's rushing tide
Walks desolate, — a widowed bride.

MAGDALENA.

I WOULD have killed you if I could,
I would have killed you where you stood,
    Magdalena.

I would have killed you if a breath
Freighted with some insensate death,
    Magdalena,

Had power to breathe your life away,
To so exhale that rose-hued clay,
    Magdalena,

That it had faded from my sight
Like roses in a single night,
    Magdalena.

I would have killed you thus, and felt
My will a blessed doom had dealt,
    Magdalena.

But who could smite that golden head,
Or mar that young cheek's perfect red,
    Magdalena?

Or pierce that bosom's tender white,
And watch those dark eyes lose their light,
    Magdalena?

Yet would to God that you were lying
Where last year's autumn leaves are dying,
    Magdalena!

Ah, would to God! then I had been
Unconscious of your scarlet sin,
    Magdalena!

Then I had never known the stain
Which purples all my life with pain,
    Magdalena;

Which robs me of my beauteous bride,
And leaves me with my stricken pride,
    Magdalena.

Ah, when I thought your soul as white
As the white rose you wore that night,
                Magdalena!

I wondered how your mother came
To give you that sin-sullied name,
                Magdalena.

Did some remorseless, vengeful Fate,
In mockery of your lofty state,
                Magdalena,

Because you wore the branded name,
Fling over you its scarlet shame,
                Magdalena?

There is no peace for you below
That horrid heritage of woe,
    Magdalena.

There is no room for you on earth,
Accurséd from your very birth,
    Magdalena.

But where the angels chant and sing,
And where the amaranth-blossoms spring,
    Magdalena,

There's room for you who have no room
Where lower angels chant your doom,
    Magdalena.

MAGDALENA.

There's room for you, the gate's ajar,
The white hands beckon from afar,
    Magdalena.

And nearer yet they stoop, they wait,
They open wide the jasper gate,
    Magdalena.

And nearer yet, — the hands stretch out,
A thousand silver trumpets shout,
    Magdalena.

They lift you up through floods of light,
I see your garments growing white,
    Magdalena.

And whiter still, *too white to touch*
The robes of us who blamed you much,
Magdalena.

AN AUTUMN BOUQUET.

BRILLIANT asters purple and gold,
 Milk-white lilies parded and pale,
With their great white petals rolled
 Fold on fold like a nun's white veil.

Sprays of geranium, leaf and flower,
 Rose-geranium in its bloom:
No strong white lily can overpower
 The rose-geranium's faint perfume.

In the centre a flash of flame,
 Slender blood-red starry slips,

AN AUTUMN BOUQUET.

With their tender tropical name,
Only made for tropical lips.

Then a girdle of brown and gold,
   Maple-leaves in their splendid death,
Starred and spotted with golden mould,
   And odorous of their dying breath.

This was the gift that into my hand
   Dropped at parting yesterday;
And the giver said, "Will you understand
   What I have said in my bouquet?"

O, your asters purple and gold,
   I read their mystical meaning well:

They symbol the world with their purple and gold,

The gay, gay world with its glittering spell!

And the lilies of peace are set beside

    The royal purples of pomp and power;

The lilies of peace and the purple of pride;

    Geranium-blooms for love in its flower.

But the fiery human heart burns on,

    Like the starry slips with their tropical name;

The fiery heart burns on and on,

    A feverish, flickering flame.

And, girdling all these pleasures and pains,

    These pleasures and passions, hopes and fears,

The solemn splendor of Death remains,

    To quench Life's laughter and tears.

THE BLACK SHAWL.

SEVEN years ago it was red
As the cactus that shed
On your bosom, last night,
Its warm crimson light.

The prettiest shawl in the world
I thought it was then, with its curled
Silken fringe, and the order
Of its prim narrow border.

Seven years it did duty;
But its bellehood and beauty

THE BLACK SHAWL.

Long since passed away,
As old and *passé*.

What hopes and what fears,
What laughter and tears,
It has long ago seen
From its rich scarlet sheen!

Seven years its hue could compare
With the flower that you wear;
Seven years it bloomed, and then *dyed*
Its soft scarlet pride.

No more like the cactus you wear,
But black as the waves of your hair;

In place of the colors so fine,

Death's sad, solemn sign.

Every thread of its rose-colored youth

Steeped in the black, bitter truth

Which comes to us all

From the grave and the pall.

But stay, — the colors of Death

Are not only for dying breath:

Let them float over life and its pride,

Over hopes that have sickened and died,

Over temples that bleed under flowers

In terrible moments and hours,

THE BLACK SHAWL.

When the thorn presses down
Through the fresh laurel crown,

Pressing out, drop by drop,
Without measure or stop,
The red costly wine
From the heart's bleeding vine.

Over homes let them wave,
Where a cold living grave
Buries peace day by day
In its dank poison clay;

Over doors where the want
Of gold brings a taunt,

And small secret stings
From a barbed arrow flings;

Over life's simplest state
Such a grim, gloomy fate,
That the heart, dumb with pain,
And too proud to complain,

Is bitterly hurled
Out, out on the world,
With faith lying dead
As a corpse in its bed;

Lying shrouded from sight,
Not in pure vestal white,

But in weeds of despair,
Black, black as your hair.

Yet memory sits
Where the black shadow flits,
And paints o'er anew
The red cactus hue,

Till in bright, bold relief
It stands out from its grief,
From its shroud and its pall,
Like the soft scarlet shawl.

JANE.

She came along the little lane,
Where all the bushes dripped with rain,
And robins sung and sung again,

As if with sudden, sheer delight,
For such a world so fresh and bright,
To swing and sing in day and night.

But, coming down the little lane,
She did not heed the robin's strain,
Nor feel the sunshine after rain.

JANE.

A little face with two brown eyes,
A little form of slender size,
A little head not very wise;

A little heart to match the head,
A foolish little heart, that bled
At every foolish word was said.

So, coming down the little lane,—
I see her now, my little Jane,—
Her foolish heart with foolish pain

Was aching, aching in her breast,
And all her pretty golden crest
Was drooping as if sore opprest.

And something, too, of anger's trace
Was on the flushed and frowning face,
And in the footsteps' quickened pace.

So swift she stept, so low she leant,
Her pretty head on thought intent,
She scarcely saw the way she went,

Nor saw the long, slim shadow fall
Across the little, low stone-wall,
As some one rose up slim and tall, —

Rose up, and came to meet her there;
A youth, with something in his air
That, at a glance, revealed his share

In all this foolish girlish pain,

This grief and anger and disdain,

That rent the heart of little Jane.

With hastier steps than hers he came,

And in a moment called her name;

And in a moment, red as flame

She blushed, and blushed, and in her eyes

A sudden, soft, and shy surprise

Did suddenly and softly rise.

"What, you?" she cried; "I thought — they said —"

Then stopped, and blushed a deeper red,

And lifted up her drooping head,

Shook back her lovely falling hair,
And arched her neck, and strove to wear
A nonchalant and scornful air.

A moment thus they held apart,
With lovers' love and lovers' art;
Then swift he caught her to his heart.

What pleasure then was born of pain,
What sunshine after cloud and rain,
As they forgave and kissed again!

'Twas April then; he talked of May,
And planned therein a wedding-day:
She blushed, but scarcely said him nay.

What pleasure now is mixed with pain,

As, looking down the little lane,

A graybeard grown, I see again,

Through twenty Aprils' rain and mist,

The little sweetheart that I kissed,

The little bride my folly missed!

PEPITA.

TENDER eyes and a thrilling voice, —
These were the lures that led me on,
Led me on to love and to trust,
Till all my heart was fairly gone.

Tender eyes and a thrilling voice!
Ah, how tender, ah, how sweet,
Eyes and voice became to me,
In the summer hours we used to meet! —

In the summer hours, in that summer land,
When I tended the vineyards day by day.

"So let me attend you from morn till night,
   Pepita, Pepita," he used to say.

Over the far blue hills he came,
   From some northern clime across the sea,
An idle stranger to spy the land,
   So I looked at him,— but he looked at me

With a lover's eyes from the very first:
   When he spoke to me his words were few,
But his voice swept through my heart like wind,
   And the vineyard seemed to blossom anew.

Tender eyes and a thrilling voice:
   Day by day and hour by hour

You held me fast in your subtle thrall,
You held me fast in your subtle power!

Tender eyes and a thrilling voice,
　The gentlest manner ever was worn,
And under it all a passionate will,
　A brooding nature set with scorn.

Tender eyes and a thrilling voice,
　Hand of steel in a velvet glove,
Together ye've wounded me full sore,
　Under the name and guise of love.

Tender eyes and a thrilling voice:
　I think of ye as I knew ye first;

Kind ye meant to be then, I know, —
To give me your best and not your worst.

Kind ye meant to be, kind ye were,
Until God knows what rose in your mind,
What ghost of ill from your shrouded past
Made you cruel, who once were kind.

Tender eyes and a thrilling voice,
I shall never see nor hear ye more;
And never forget, though I've long forgiven,
The hurt that left me wounded and sore.

THE GARDEN OF THE LILIES.

It is the time of the lilies;
  Look down in the garden there,
At the white bride-blossoms swinging
  Bloom-censers into the air;
At the white bride-blossoms flinging
  Their odors into the air.

The sky is a sea of sapphire,
  Dappled with purple and gold;
White heats from the heart of August
  Over the land are rolled, —

White heats from the heart of August
Into the lilies fold.

Into the death-white lilies,
Down in the garden there,
The hundred lilies ringing
Bloom-bells in the ardent air, —
The hundred lilies ringing
A requiem of despair.

The days are a swoon of silence,
A drowsy dream of death;
But at eve a wind comes blowing
A sweet southwestern breath;
At eve a wind comes blowing
Up from a river of Death.

THE GARDEN OF THE LILIES.

At the foot of the garden there
It sleeps all day in the sun;
A river of amethyst veiled with mist,
Till the swoon of the day is done;
A river of amethyst veiled with mist,
Which the white bride-lilies shun.

From what far mystical islands,
Over what strange sea-floors,
Does the southwest-wind come blowing
Into these lonely shores?
Does the southwest-wind come blowing
An echo of ghostly oars?

There's something astir on the grass,
Just under the lilies there,

A glitter of white in the dim midnight,
 And a sudden chill in the air;
A glitter of white in the August night,
 And a throbbing thrill in the air.

The lilies shiver and sigh,
 The lilies murmur and moan,
With a tender, tremulous thrill,
 In their wild Æolian tone;
A tender, tremulous thrill,
 As she stands there all alone.

Did she step from the lilies down,
 A splendid spirit of bloom,
With a shimmer of amber tresses flung
 Like a meteor into the gloom?

A shimmer of amber tresses flung

   Into the midnight gloom?

Did she step from the lilies down,

   This shape of a womanly grace,

With an awful beauty shining clear

   Out of her phantom face?

An awful beauty shining clear

   From the light of her phantom face?

The murk of the midnight gloom

   With a pallid radiance glows,

As she glides like a meteor down to the strand

   At the foot of the garden close;

As she glides like a meteor down to the strand

   Where the river of amethyst flows.

A mystical murmur breaks

    From the waves that break on the shore,

And a phantom boat drops dreamily down

    To the dip of a ghostly oar;

A phantom boat drops dreamily down,

    And never comes back to shore.

She sits at the slender stern,

    The queen of a ghostly realm,

While a pennon of amber flutters and floats

    Away from the shadowy helm;

A pennon of amber tresses floats

    Away from the dusky helm.

What is it she seeks in the night?

    What ghostly tryst doth she keep

THE GARDEN OF THE LILIES.

At the foot of the garden there,

    While the earth lies shrouded in sleep, —

At the foot of the garden there

    What terrible tryst doth she keep?

O, ask of the pale sighing lilies,

    What secret of solemn despair

Lies hid in their white bridal bosoms,

    And lurks in the chill haunted air, —

Lying hid in their beautiful bosoms,

    What secret of solemn despair!

IN AN HOUR.

I.

ANTICIPATION.

"I'LL take the orchard path," she said,
    Speaking lowly, smiling slowly:
The brook was dried within its bed,
The hot sun flung a flame of red
Low in the west as forth she sped.

Across the dried brook-course she went,
    Singing lowly, smiling slowly;
She scarcely felt the sun that spent

Its fiery force in swift descent,
She never saw the wheat was bent,

The grasses parched, the blossoms dried;
Singing lowly, smiling slowly,
Her eyes amidst the drouth espied
A summer pleasance far and wide,
With roses and sweet violets pied.

II.

DISAPPOINTMENT.

But homeward coming all the way,
Sighing lowly, pacing slowly,
She knew the bent wheat withering lay,
She saw the blossoms' dry decay,
She missed the little brooklet's play.

A breeze had sprung from out the south,
    But, sighing lowly, pacing slowly,
She only felt the burning drouth;
Her eyes were hot and parched her mouth,
Yet sweet the wind blew from the south.

And when the wind brought welcome rain,
    Still sighing lowly, pacing slowly,
She never saw the lifting grain,
But only — a lone orchard lane,
Where she had waited all in vain.

UPHARSIN.

SCENA.—In a Vienna palace when the news is brought of the fall of Sebastopol.

OVER the city a shadowy cloud
Floated and floated; a gloomy gray shroud,
Floating from cannon-shot, gun-shot, and shell,
Thicker and thicker the dense shadow fell.

Into the palace it stealthily comes,
With the sound of the trumpet, the rolling of drums,
And the glittering guests in the glittering dance
Hear with it the sound of the shivering lance;

But never the cries of the wounded and dying,

Who drop in the trenches, or fall in their flying;

For the Redan, the Redan, is taken at last,

And Sebastopol falters before the death-blast.

Yet gay in the palace their glasses are clinking,

And merry lips laugh o'er the wine they are drinking.

But there's blood, crimson blood, in the rose-rippled tide,

And the lips that are laughing are laughing to hide

The quiver and shiver of hearts that await

But the sound of *their* trumpet to challenge the fate

Which lies in the splendor of Austria's palace,
Like death in the depths of a rose-crested chalice.

O Tyranny, pause in your soft, silken bower,
And list to the wild, throbbing hearts in this hour!
They're athirst, all athirst, and 't is blood that
    they quaff,
Your blood which they drink with that merry,
    low laugh!

And it drips from their lips to the white marble
    floor,
And the rich silver service seems dabbled with
    gore;
But you hear not, you see not: the laugh and the
    jest
Drown the curse of the gallant Hungarian guest.

But the sound of the trumpet, the rolling of drums,

Through the laugh and the jest to Hungary comes;

While "The Kaiser, the Kaiser is taken at last,

And Austria yields before the death-blast!"

Is the cry that they hear coming nearer and nearer,

As the sound of the trumpet comes clearer and clearer,

With the ringing of Victory's sweet marriage-bell,

Through the booming of cannon-shot, gun-shot, and shell.

YESTERNIGHT.

THE memories of yesternight,
   When in that swift, bewildering dance,
   The pressure of your hand, your glance,
All thrill me with a new delight.

The music wrapped us round and round,
   While thus within the waltz we whirled,
   Regardless of the crowd, the world ;
The music wrapped us round and round.

And, listening to the quickened beat
   Of hearts that beat a wilder tune

Than horn and harp and gay bassoon,
We floated on with tireless feet.

A thousand odors filled the air, —
　Swept o'er us as we swept along,
　Through all the mazy moving throng;
A thousand odors, wondrous rare,

Swept o'er us from a thousand flowers,
　At every breathing of the breeze,
　From lime and pomegranate trees,
And orange in the orange bowers.

From lilies with their creamy flush,
　All splendors of the splendid rose,

Musk, moss, and cinnamon, in blows
And buds of crimson, white, and blush.

But more delicious than the scent
   Of Orient shrub or orange-bloom,
   The warm and subtly sweet perfume
Which in your breathing came and went;

Your breath, so soft and balmy sweet,
   That touched my cheek, that stirred my hair,
   That wandered o'er and o'er me there,
As faster fell our flying feet.

As faster, faster on, until
   Beyond the long and gay saloon

YESTERNIGHT.

We stood alone, beneath the moon,
In garden alleys, dusk and still.

The lights are out, and coldly through
   The deepening dawn the day begins;
   But still I hear the violins,
And still in dreams I waltz with you.

AN ACQUAINTANCE.

I REMEMBER when first we met;
I think I shall never forget
The drawing-room in its curtained gloom,
The amber-curtained drawing-room,

Which set you round like a frame of gold,
As out of the December cold
You hurried in, with your bright blond skin,
A splendid color from cheek to chin.

And, sitting down by my cousin Jane,
You sipped the foam from the pink champagne,

While over the wine the shimmer and shine
Of your strange eyes kept haunting mine.

You talked to her, but you looked at me ;
Such a curious gaze, — what did you see,
What did you trace within my face,
As you drank and talked with that smiling grace?

Always that nonchalant smiling grace,
Always a mask drawn over the face,
Always a look as if within
You guarded a secret sorrow or sin.

HER SECRET.

What if I think of you once in a while,
With a little blush and a little smile;
With a little blush that comes and goes
As the sweet, sweet wind of memory blows?

What if I picture now with care
A tête-à-tête and an easy-chair?
What if I make the picture clear,
By lighting it up with a chandelier?

Can you see by the softly shimmering flame, —
Can you see to read the musical name

HER SECRET.

Of him who sits in graceful state
On the little damask tête-à-tête?

Can you see me sitting before him there,
Sitting within the easy-chair?
Can you hear the laugh, can you hear the jest,
The musical laugh of my handsome guest?

Is it unwise to paint the view
In colors so warm, — and light it too?
Will somebody claim the graceful state
On the little damask tête-à-tête?

How many may lose by claiming that!
For many a handsome guest has sat

Beneath the shimmering chandelier,

While the easy-chair was standing near.

How many may lose, how many may win!

Ah, vanity is a costly sin!

For the one I mean will never suppose

That for him the wind of memory blows.

Then what if I think of you once in a while,

With a little blush and a little smile;

With a little blush that comes and goes

As the sweet, sweet wind of memory blows!

JENNY.

Little Jenny, pretty Jenny,
  Jenny with the perfect eyes,
Jenny with the soft silk hair,
  And the red mouth puckered wise.

Little Jenny, pretty Jenny,
  Jenny with her charming ways,
Jenny with her wooing smiles,
  And her broken R's and A's.

Little Jenny, pretty Jenny,
  Jenny with that perfect form,

Jenny with that mingled temper,
Half of sunshine, half of storm.

Little Jenny, pretty Jenny,
  Laughing as you strive to catch her,
When you chase her round the room, —
  Ah! what baby e'er can match her?

Little Jenny, Carrie's Jenny;
  There was never such another
As this baby, save, it may be,
  Listen, Carrie, — Jenny's mother.

Little Jenny, matchless Jenny,
  Sunshine kiss her, winds caress her,
Dark-browed sorrow, do not touch her,
  Or, if touching, touch to bless her.

TWO VIEWS.

"The world is old, the world is cold,"
  She very coldly said,
"And all we prize beyond us lies
  Till we lie with the dead.

"The world is old, the world is cold;
  A thousand lives can prove
How failures cast us all at last
  Into the worldly groove."

A thousand lives are not my life,
  Nor are they types of mine;

Instead of cold, the world is gold,
And dazzles with its shine.

She shook her head, she broke her thread,
And paused to count the stitches;
And still she told, the world was cold,
And colder all its riches.

And still I hold the world is gold,
And golden all its glory;
And still she sings of "fleeting things,"
That dismal, dreary story.

The daisies blow, the roses grow,
In garden, field, and wood,

And care is fleet, where youth is sweet,

And God is very good.

I still must weave, and still believe

My dreams will all come true;

For hope is bright, and sorrow light,

Where life is fresh and new.

HAUNTED.

You ask me why my thoughts assume
Such dark significance of gloom,
When, sitting in the chapel there,
I list the sermon and the prayer.

If you could summon up such hosts
Of phantom figures, dreary ghosts,
That come and take their seat beside
My seat, or in the stillness glide

Along the purple-tinted aisle,
And whisper of the past, the while

The preacher prays his solemn prayer,

You would not wonder at me there.

If you could hear the tones, my friend,

That with the singers' voices blend,

Or when the organ thunders roll, —

You would not question thus my soul.

You would not wonder that I turn

From church and chapel with so stern

A sadness on my outward face,

And thus refuse your gentle grace.

HESTER BROWNE.

O, you are charming, Hester Browne,
So do not, every time you pass
The little Psyche looking-glass,
Find some disorder in your gown!

In every ringlet of your hair,
   In every dimple of your cheek,
   Whene'er you smile or smiling speak,
There lurks a cruel, charming snare.

There's not a motion of the hand
   That shows a grace to lure and win,

There's not a coy, coquettish sin,
That Hester does not understand.

What use to preach of "better things,"
   And tell her she is false as gay?
   Be still, and let her have her day,
And count her lovers on her rings.

And let her break a hundred hearts,
   And mend them with a glance again ;
   Be sure the pleasure heals the pain
Of little Hester's cruel arts.

DESTINY.

Just a door between us, — no more,
And your hand on the bell,
When a voice inside of the door
    Broke the spell.

And you turned, perhaps with a sigh,
  From the small garden gate,
And I never knew you were by
    Till too late.

So near, so near, yet so far!
  Just a thin narrow door
Shut between us, — just a far
    Evermore!

And now, perhaps with a sigh,
    Or a smile, — who can tell? —
I think what we missed, you and I,
        For that bell.

God knew best, though when your last letter
    Told the story to me,
For a time, I thought I knew better,
        For you see

I wanted what there was denied,
    Were it a weed or a flower;
I wanted what budded and died
        In that hour.

And though I look back on that season
    Of friendship platonic,
And laugh at the rhyme without reason,
        Half ironic;

And though time has brought me far more
    Than I care now to tell,
I sometimes think of that door
            And that bell!

LOSS AND GAIN.

When the baby died, we said,
With a sudden, secret dread,
"Death, be merciful, and pass;
Leave the other." But, alas,

While we watched he waited there,
One foot on the golden stair,
One hand beckoning at the gate,
Till the home was desolate.

Friends say, it is better so,
Clothed in innocence to go;

Say, to ease your parting pain,
That your loss is but their gain.

Ah, the parents think of this,
But remember more the kiss
From the little rose-red lips!
And the print of finger-tips

Left upon a broken toy
Will remind them how the boy
And his sister charmed the days
With their pretty winsome ways.

Only time can give relief
To the weary, lonesome grief;
God's sweet minister of pain
Then shall sing of loss and gain.

HOMELESS.

O, THE wild, wild trouble in your eye,
  Marghrita!
The sad, sad trouble that doth lie
  Beyond the reaching
  Of all preaching,
  Marghrita.
Of the dark, dark days you spend,
  Marghrita, —
The dreary, lonesome days that rend
  You with their woe,
  What do they know,
  Marghrita,

Who stand amid the flowers of life,
   Marghrita,
And have no knowledge of the strife
   Which leaves its trace
   Upon your face,
   Marghrita?
No matter if the winds blow east or west,
   Marghrita;
They have pleasant homes wherein to rest,
   While you have none
   Under the sun,
   Marghrita.

LA SIRÈNE.

Over the flagon filled to the brim
She sends a bewildering glance to him.

Over the sea of pink foaming wine
He reels in the light of her beauty divine.

Deeper and deeper she dreamily dips,
In the rose-tinted wine, her rose-tinted lips.

While over the glass she airily laughs
A pledge which he eagerly catches and quaffs.

And he drinks in a madness wilder than wine,
Through her smile and her eyes' bewildering shine.

He drinks in delirium, danger, and death,
As over the crystal comes floating her breath;

As over the flagon of rose-colored bliss
She wickedly, witchingly wafts him a kiss;

Then, laughing a laugh derisive and sweet,
She is gone while he kneels in despair at her feet.

TYING HER BONNET UNDER HER CHIN.

TYING her bonnet under her chin,
She tied her raven ringlets in ;
But not alone in the silken snare
Did she catch her lovely floating hair,
For, tying her bonnet under her chin,
She tied a young man's heart within.

They were strolling together up the hill,
Where the wind comes blowing merry and chill ;
And it blew the curls, a frolicsome race,
All over the happy peach-colored face,

Till, scolding and laughing, she tied them in,
Under her beautiful dimpled chin.

And it blew a color, bright as the bloom
Of the pinkest fuschia's tossing plume,
All over the cheeks of the prettiest girl
That ever imprisoned a romping curl,
Or, tying her bonnet under her chin,
Tied a young man's heart within.

Steeper and steeper grew the hill;
Madder, merrier, chillier still
The western wind blew down, and played
The wildest tricks with the little maid,
As, tying her bonnet under her chin,
She tied a young man's heart within.

O western wind, do you think it was fair,

To play such tricks with her floating hair?

To gladly, gleefully do your best

To blow her against the young man's breast,

Where he as gladly folded her in,

And kissed her mouth and her dimpled chin?

Ah! Ellery Vane, you little thought,

An hour ago, when you besought

This country lass to walk with you,

After the sun had dried the dew,

What perilous danger you'd be in,

As she tied her bonnet under her chin!

THAT WALTZ OF VON WEBER'S.

GAYLY and gayly rang the gay music,
The blithe, merry music of harp and of horn,
The mad, merry music, that set us a-dancing
Till over the midnight came stealing the morn.

Down the great hall went waving the banners,
Waving and waving their red, white, and blue,
As the sweet summer wind came blowing and
 blowing
From the city's great gardens asleep in the
 dew.

Under the flags, as they floated and floated,
Under the arches and arches of flowers,
We two and we two floated and floated
Into the mystical midnight hours.

And just as the dawn came stealing and stealing,
The last of those wild Weber waltzes began;
I can hear the soft notes now appealing and
  pleading,
And I catch the faint scent of the sandal-wood
  fan

That lay in your hand, your hand on my shoulder,
As down the great hall, away and away,
All under the flags and under the arches,
We danced and we danced till the dawn of the
  day.

But why should I dream o'er this dreary old
  ledger,
In this counting-room down in this dingy old street,
Of that night or that morning, just there at the
  dawning,
When our hearts beat in time to our fast-flying
  feet?

What is it that brings me that scene of enchant-
  ment,
So fragrant and fresh from out the dead years,
That just for a moment I 'd swear that the music
Of Weber's wild waltzes were still in my ears?

What is it, indeed, in this dusty old alley,
That brings me that night or that morning in June?

What is it, indeed? — I laugh to confess it, —
A hand-organ grinding a creaking old tune!

But somewhere or other I caught in the measure
That waltz of Von Weber's, and back it all came,
That night or that morning, just there at the
    dawning,
When I danced the last dance with my first and
    last flame.

My first and my last! but who would believe me
If, down in this dusty old alley to-day,
'Twixt the talk about cotton, the markets, and
    money,
I should suddenly turn in some moment and say

That one memory only had left me a lonely

And gray-bearded bachelor, dreaming of Junes,

Where the nights and the mornings, from the dusk to the dawnings,

Seemed set to the music of Weber's wild tunes?

HALF AN HOUR.

I MET her last year, in the studio
    Of Weymer, in the Rue de Charente;
She came in with cheeks all aglow
    From the wild autumn winds, and bent
To my greetings with a flow

Of light murmured words, silver sweet,
    Delicate, flattering phrases,
Which my own words sprang forth to meet,
    As if I believed in her praises,
Dropped with a smile at my feet.

Courtesy, high-handed, and bred
  In the translucent blood of her veins:
Such a lady! who can flatter, instead
  Of your flattering her for your pains,
Without a change of her cool white and red.

Saying, "I've heard of you much" —
  Smiling — "and glad thus to meet";
While her hand's tender touch
  Brushed my own, to complete
The chaste charm: call it such,

.For I knew that it meant nothing more
  Than the gracious refinement of art;
The exquisite odorous core
  Of a flower, not its heart.
What wanted I more?

The flower itself for my share?
   Well, I have it here in my palm, —
A rose that fell from her hair
   Into my hand, like a charm,
Just as we parted there.

And half smiling I took it away, —
   Half smiling, but was I in jest?
Well, what next? shall I say
   I have worn it here on my breast
Since that red autumn day?

Only the swift short half
   Of a long-drawn hour,
An arch phrase or two, and a laugh:
   What *is* the power? —
Did she give me wine to quaff?

For, ever I'm seeing a face,
    Like a face in a delicate dream.
Larkspur eyes and rose lips through the lace
    Of a veil glide and gleam,
Till I half lose the trace.

Then a turn of the head shows such hair!
    Black hair like wet silk,
Breaking loose from a silken snare,
    And a hand white as milk
Thrusting it back without care.

More than a year, you know,
    And much has happened since then;
The world's ebb-tide and flow,
    And a man's life with men;
But I'd let it all go

HALF AN HOUR.

For the swift short half
  Of a long-drawn hour,
An arch phrase or two, and a laugh,
  And the possible power
To sit there and quaff

That fine fairy wine,
  Which has kept its sweet spell,
Kept its sparkle and shine,
  Down a year's surge and swell,
From that half-hour of mine.

Of mine! yes, of mine, sweet!
  You've met millions of men,
And dropped a smile at their feet;
  But that half-hour was mine then,
And in it I claim you, sweet.

And in it I have you and hold you,
Larkspur eyes and blush roses!
And in it I clasp you and fold you,
Where this rose reposes.
There, my passion I've told you!

POLLY.

Who's this coming down the stairs,
Putting on such lofty airs;
With that hump upon her back,
And her little heels click, clack?
Such a funny little girl,
With a funny great long curl
Hanging from a mound of hair;
And a hat way back in the air,
Just to show a little border
Of yellow curls, all out of order.
She's a silly girl, I guess,
I'm glad it is n't — Why, bless

My soul! it's our little Polly
Tricked out in all that folly!
Well, I declare, I never
Was so beat; for if ever
There was a sensible girl,
I thought 't was little Polly Earl.
And here — Well, it's very queer
To come back, after a year,
And find my Polly changed like this, —
A hunched-up, bunched-up, furbelowed miss,
With a steeple of a hat,
And her hair like a mat,
It's so frightfully frowzled
And roughed up and tousled!
O Polly, Polly! — Well, my dear,
So you're glad grandfather's here?

And I confess that kiss

Does *smack* of the Polly I miss, —

The girl with the soft, smooth hair,

Instead of this kinked-up snare.

What! you 're just the same Polly,

In spite of all this folly?

And what is that you say

About your grandmother's day,

That you guess the folly

Has n't just begun? — O Polly,

If you could only have seen

Your grandmother at eighteen!

What 's that about the puffs

And the stiffened-up ruffs

That they wore in the time

Of your grandmother's prime?

And the big buckram sleeves
That stood out like the leaves
Of the old-fashioned tables;
And the bonnets big as gables,
And the laced-up waists — Why, sho,
Polly, how your tongue does go!
Little girls should be seen, not heard
Quite so much, Polly, on my word.
O, I'm trying to get away,
Eh, from your grandmother's day,
But I'm not to escape
Quite so easy from a scrape?
What, you expect me to say
That your grandmother's day
Was as foolish as this? —
Polly, give me a kiss;

I 'm beaten, I see —
And I 'll agree, I 'll agree
That young folks find
All things to their mind;
And in your grandmother's time,
When I too was in my prime,
I 've no doubt, Polly,
I looked at all the folly
Connected with the lasses
Through rose-colored glasses,
As the youths of to-day
Look at you, Polly, eh?
But I 've given you fair warning
How older folk see; so, Polly, good morning!

BESS AND BEN.

SUNNY days, and sunny days,
    And all day long,
Here they go, and there they go,
    In and out the throng.

Here they go, and there they go,
    Up and down the street;
Benjie grinding out the tune,
    Bessie singing sweet.

Singing loud, and singing low,
    Trilling out the tune,

Not as Benjie grinds it out,
  But as birds in June

Lift and lift their voices up
  Out of pure delight;
Singing loud, and singing low,
  Morning, noon, and night.

What! you never heard our Bess?
  Never heard her sing
"John Brown's soul is marching on,"
  And "The Lord is King"?

Why, where've you lived, I wonder,
  Never to have heard

Bessie, with her tambourine,
Singing like a bird?

Singing up and down the street,
Singing high and low,
Since a little child of three,
Twice three years ago.

It is twice three years, and more,
Since that summer day
When the news from Gettysburg
Told how Sergeant May,

Through the thickest of the fight,
Through the rush and roar

BESS AND BEN.

Of the shout and shot and shell,
   Held the flag he bore

Firmly, till the very last,
   When they found him lying
By the famous old stone-wall,
   In the twilight, — dying.

Dying, faltering at the last,
   "Little Bess and Ben!
They'll miss their father sorely:
   Who'll look out for them when—"

And that was all, — the words broke off
   In this world, for the other,

And little Bess and Ben were left
With neither father, mother.

And this is why that through the street,
In and out the throng,
Sunny days and sunny days,
And all day long,

Here they go, and there they go,
Up and down the street;
Benjie grinding out the tune,
Bessie singing sweet.

BLANCHE'S CHÂTEAUX.

BUILDING castles in the air,

Spanish castles, fine and fair,

Blanche is dreaming in her chair ;

 Keep on dreaming, Blanche.

Poverty is on the wall,

And its shadows downward fall

Drearily upon them all,

 But the dreaming Blanche.

While they mourn their scanty fare,

And their daily toil and care,

She is ever dreaming there;
    Keep on dreaming, Blanche.

While they chide thee in disdain,
For thy heedlessness of pain,
Thou art having all the gain,
    In thy dreaming, Blanche.

While they only see their cot,
Bounded by its narrow lot,
Scant domains are heeded not
    By the dreaming Blanche.

She is wandering far away, —
Building castles grand and gay, —

Growing grander every day ;
   Keep on dreaming, Blanche.

Stately mansions, — there they stand,
In Atlantis fairy-land,
By delicious breezes fanned ;
   Keep on dreaming, Blanche.

Ocean surges rise and fall
'Neath the turrets slim and tall,
'Gainst a battlemented wall,
   In thy dreaming, Blanche.

Where the summer shadows hide,
On the sunny southern side,

There a garden stretches wide, —
There is dreaming Blanche.

Friends of rare and costly mien,
Such as we have never seen,
In that Paradise serene,
Walk with dreaming Blanche.

Blanche is queen in these domains;
Blanche o'er all this beauty reigns,
And a queenly state sustains;
Keep thy dreaming, Blanche.

Though they tell thee how unreal
Are these visions, and ideal,

I will tell thee they are real,
    And to keep on dreaming.

I will tell thee, for I know
How their splendors come and go,
That the truest life we know
    Is in dreaming, Blanche.

In our fair Atlantis land
We have riches at command,
Which they cannot understand:
    Let us dream forever.

APPLE-BLOSSOMS.

HITHER and thither they swung, Madeline Hays,—
 The bloom-loaded apple-tree boughs,
 The rose-scented apple-tree boughs,
 The pink-tinted apple-tree boughs,—
In the merry May days.

Hither and thither they swung, Madeline Hays;
 The blossoms and you together,
 Rose-tinted, and light as a feather,
 All in the merry May weather,
My rose-tinted Madeline Hays.

Down in the wet, green grass, Madeline Hays,
  Where the brown bees cluster and hover;
  Down in the cowslips and clover,
  With the apple-tree blooms sprinkled over,
I awaited you, Madeline Hays.

Down in the wet, green grass, Madeline Hays,
  Ankle-deep, I pleaded and flattered,
  While the blackbird whistled and chattered,
  And the pink blossoms pelted and pattered,
All in the merry May days.

"Come down, come down to me, Madeline Hays!"
  I pleaded, and pleaded in vain;
  While the pink, pelting rain
  And your laugh of disdain
Only answered me, Madeline Hays.

"Come down, come down to me, Madeline Hays!"
    I pleaded, and flattered once more;
    And you laughed in my face as before,
    Till the wind blew down with a roar!—
What happened then, Madeline Hays?

The wind blew down with a roar, Madeline Hays,
    Breaking branches and boughs in the race,
    Blowing blossoms and buds in my face;
    What else did I catch and embrace
As the bough broke, Madeline Hays?

Soft, yellow silk hair, Madeline Hays,
    Unrolling its lovely Greek twist,
    Blowing out its goldening mist,—
    It was this that I caught first and kissed,
My bloom-blushing Madeline Hays!

Then through hair all a-dazzle, Madeline Hays,

Eyes and mouth, cheek and chin too,

Out of the dazzle came glimmering through;

All the love colors, — red, white, and blue, —

What could a man do, Madeline Hays?

IN JUNE.

So sweet, so sweet the roses in their blowing,
  So sweet the daffodils, so fair to see;
So blithe and gay the humming-bird a-going
  From flower to flower, a-hunting with the bee.

So sweet, so sweet the calling of the thrushes,
  The calling, cooing, wooing, everywhere;
So sweet the water's song through reeds and rushes,
  The plover's piping note, now here, now there.

So sweet, so sweet from off the fields of clover,
  The west-wind blowing, blowing up the hill;

So sweet, so sweet with news of some one's lover,
    Fleet footsteps, ringing nearer, nearer still.

So near, so near, now listen, listen, thrushes;
    Now plover, blackbird, cease, and let me hear;
And, water, hush your song through reeds and
        rushes,
    That I may know whose lover cometh near.

So loud, so loud the thrushes kept their calling,
    Plover or blackbird never heeding me;
So loud the mill-stream too kept fretting, falling,
    O'er bar and bank, in brawling, boisterous glee.

So loud, so loud; yet blackbird, thrush, nor plover,
    Nor noisy mill-stream, in its fret and fall,

Could drown the voice, the low voice of my lover,
   My lover calling through the thrushes' call.

"Come down, come down!" he called, and straight
      the thrushes
   From mate to mate sang all at once, "Come
      down!"
And while the water laughed through reeds and
      rushes,
   The blackbird chirped, the plover piped, "Come
      down!"

Then down and off, and through the fields of clover,
   I followed, followed, at my lover's call;
Listening no more to blackbird, thrush, or plover,
   The water's laugh, the mill-stream's fret and fall.

ANOTHER YEAR.

"ANOTHER year," she said, "another year
These roses I have watched with so much care,
Have watched and tended without pain or fear,
Shall bud and bloom for me exceeding fair,—
Another year," she said, "another year."

"Another year," she said, "another year,
My life, perhaps, may bud and bloom again,
May bud and bloom like these red roses here,
Unlike them, tended with regret and pain,—
Another year, perhaps, another year.

"Another year, ah yes, another year,

When bloom my roses, all my life shall bloom;

When summer comes, my summer too 'll be here,

And I shall cease to wander in this gloom,—

Another year, ah yes, another year.

"For ah, another year, another year,

I 'll set my life in richer, stronger soil,

And prune the weeds away that creep too near,

And watch and tend with never-ceasing toil,—

Another year, ah yes, another year."

Another year, alas! another year,

The roses all lay withering ere their prime,

Poor blighted buds, with scanty leaves and sere,

Drooping and dying long before their time,—

Another year, alas! another year.

And ah, another year, another year,

Low, like the blighted dying buds, she lay,

Whose voice had prophesied without a fear,

Whose hand had trimmed the rose-tree day by day,

To bloom another year, another year.

SOME DAY OF DAYS.

Some day, some day of days, threading the street
    With idle, heedless pace,
    Unlooking for such grace,
    I shall behold your face!
Some day, some day of days, thus may we meet.

Perchance the sun may shine from skies of May,
    Or winter's icy chill
    Touch whitely vale and hill.
    What matter? I shall thrill
Through every vein with summer on that day.

Once more life's perfect youth will all come back,
    And for a moment there
    I shall stand fresh and fair,
    And drop the garment care;
Once more my perfect youth will nothing lack.

I shut my eyes now, thinking how 't will be, —
    How face to face each soul
    Will slip its long control,
    Forget the dismal dole
Of dreary Fate's dark separating sea;

And glance to glance, and hand to hand in greeting,
    The past with all its fears,
    Its silences and tears,
    Its lonely, yearning years,
Shall vanish in the moment of that meeting.

CECILY.

"O, IF my love would come to me,
Would come to me and speak to me
Out of these shadows dark and dree,
My heart would so much lighter be,
My heart would so much lighter be!"
    Sang Cecily, sad Cecily.

"O, if my love would come to me,
And say the words he said to me
Another day, for love of me,
The world would so much brighter be,

The world so much brighter be!"

Sang fair, deserted Cecily.

"O, if my love would come to me,

And hold my hands and look at me,

The while he softly spoke to me,

My life would so much brighter be,

My life would so much brighter be!"

Despairingly sang Cecily.

"But silent and away from me,

He has no word of cheer for me,

For one dark day he doubted me,

And doubting me, grew hard to me,

And doubting me grew hard to me,"

Half bitterly sang Cecily.

K

"But O, if he would come to me,
Just for a little while to me,
Before he left me, he should see
That I was true as truth could be,
That I was true as truth could be!"
    Sang tenderly sweet Cecily.

"O, if he would but come to me
For long enough to learn of me
This precious truth, and say to me
The words he said before to me,
For love of me, for love of me,"
    Sang Cecily, fair Cecily,

"My way would so much brighter be,
My cross would so much lighter be;

And patiently I'd wait and see
Whatever was in store for me,
Whatever was in store for me,"
    Sang wistfully poor Cecily.

"But now through shadows dark and dree
He will not help me, who might be
A rock amidst this surging sea,
A shield between the world and me,
A shield between the world and me,"
    Sang tearfully sad Cecily.

"And all I ask to comfort me,
Is that he'll come once more to me,
And say the words he said to me
Another day, for love of me,

Another day, for love of me,"

    Sang pleadingly sweet Cecily.

"Yet though these shadows dark and dree
Grow dark and darker yet to see,
I will not doubt, as he doubts me,
But still believe he'll come to me,
But still believe he'll come to me!"

    With sudden cheer

      Sang high and clear

        This fond and faithful Cecily.

RIDING DOWN.

O, DID you see him riding down,
And riding down, while all the town
Came out to see, came out to see,
And all the bells rang mad with glee?

O, did you hear those bells ring out,
The bells ring out, the people shout,
And did you hear that cheer on cheer
That over all the bells rang clear?

And did you see the waving flags,
The fluttering flags, the tattered flags,

Red, white, and blue, shot through and through,
Baptized with battle's deadly dew?

And did you hear the drums' gay beat,
The drums' gay beat, the bugles sweet,
The cymbals' clash, the cannons' crash,
That rent the sky with sound and flash?

And did you see me waiting there,
Just waiting there and watching there,
One little lass, amid the mass
That pressed to see the hero pass?

And did you see him smiling down,
And smiling down, as riding down

With slowest pace, with stately grace,

He caught the vision of a face, —

My face uplifted red and white,

Turned red and white with sheer delight,

To meet the eyes, the smiling eyes,

Outflashing in their swift surprise?

O, did you see how swift it came,

How swift it came, like sudden flame,

That smile to me, to only me,

The little lass who blushed to see?

And at the windows all along,

O all along, a lovely throng

Of faces fair, beyond compare,
Beamed out upon him riding there!

Each face was like a radiant gem,
A sparkling gem, and yet for them
No swift smile came, like sudden flame,
No arrowy glance took certain aim.

He turned away from all their grace,
From all that grace of perfect face,
He turned to me, to only me,
The little lass who blushed to see!

SOMEBODY'S HUMMING-BIRD.

IN gay groves once you sped
   On glancing wing,
Or dipped your gleaming head
   In many a spring,
      Dew-welling
      And up-swelling
   From roses red.

Or in some garden fair,
   Or glen remote,
While flitting here and there,
   You hummed your note

Of pleasure,
For the measure
Of days so rare.

But on no bending bough
In gay green grove,
Or flowery garden now,
You flit and rove,
Sweet comer
Of the summer.
Shall I tell how

Your little feet find rest,
Your wings repose,
Within a golden nest,
Where neither rose

Nor lily,
White and chilly,
Hideth your breast?

A nest, that's like a throne
Upon a bower,
Where, reigning all alone,
Without a flower
To kiss there,
You never miss there
The brightest rose that's blown.

Where fixt and fast you swing,
Half poised for flight,
On stirless, heedless wing,
Night after night,

While harpers play,
And dancers gay
Through merry measures swing.

Through merry measures, where
A girl's face glances
Beneath its golden hair,
As down the dances
Her twinkling feet
To swift tunes beat,
While you above there,

O ruby-throated Hummer,
In your bower,
Forgetful of the summer
In its flower,

Caught in a snare
Of golden hair,
Watch each new-comer,

With eyes wide and unwinking
In their brightness,
And little head unthinking
Of the slightness
Of its hold
Upon the gold
Gay tresses, overlinking

Curl on curl, round a face,
Rising fair,
Like a lily in its grace,
Or a rare

Blush rose,

When it blows

From the green bud's embrace.

But rose or lily rare,

She has caught you

In a gay golden snare,

And has taught you,

Little Hummer,

That the summer,

Though so fair,

May spread many a net

For unheeding

Little rovers, who forget

Where they 're speeding,

Until, lo !
Ere they know,
They are set

Fast forever in a snare, —
Be its name
Lily, rose, or golden hair,
All 's the same.
So, gay Hummers
Of the summers
Yet to come, — beware !

SYLVIA'S SONG.

THE days are sweet and long,—oh! sweet and
    long;
All day I sit and dream, or sing the song
That some one sang for me one summer day,
For me, to me, before he went his way.

The days are sweet and long,—oh! sweet and
    long;
And in the sun I sit, and sing my song:
Some day he will come back who went away,
And sing the song I sing from day to day.

SYLVIA'S SONG.

The days are long, but sweet, — oh! long, but sweet;
Some day I'll hear the music of his feet
Who sang for me, and sang my heart away,
My happy heart, — before he went his way.

Some day, — to-day, perhaps, — he'll come to me;
And then the days, so long, but sweet to me,
Will lose the burden of "So long, so long!"
And only keep the sweet of all the song.

THORNS.

Who sees the thorns beneath the crown,
    Upon a poet's head?
Who knows they sometimes sing to drown
    Some horrid, haunting dread?

Who knows what fears beset their way?
    Who knows, who cares indeed,
So sweetness charms within the lay,
    That aching temples bleed?

Who knows how much they long to shrink
    Misfortune's cruel cup?

Who knows what bitter wine they drink,

Who drain that poison up?

Ah, never say the poet writes

The sweeter for his pain;

'T is false! the dying soldier fights,

A bloody field to gain.

"AND A LITTLE CHILD SHALL LEAD THEM."

WHERE? into the trifles of life?
Into its folly and sin?
Into its madness and strife,
Shall the little child lead you in?

Into jealousy, envy, and hate,
And the soul's surest wrong,
Which lies in that bitter estate,
Shall the little child lead you along?

Think of the birthright that's yours!
Yours, whom Christ died to save!

Think of the world that endures,

Beyond the dead and the grave!

In view of that wonderful land

Where your inheritance lies,

In view of a little child's hand

To lead you on to the prize,

Think, think if you can of the world's purple glory!

Of its jealousy, envy, and hate,

And add if you can to the old, wicked story,

In view of that splendid estate!

In view of the child, that is waiting to lead

From the misery, madness, and scorn,

O, add if you can, to temples that bleed,

Another sharp, cruel thorn!

WHAT MAY BE.

WHEN the days are longer, longer,
And the sun shines stronger, stronger,
And the winds cease blowing, blowing,
And the winter's chance of snowing
  Is lost in springtime weather;

And the brooks start running, running,
And the bee sits sunning, sunning,
And the birds come, bringing, bringing,
Such good news in their singing
  Of love and springtime weather;

WHAT MAY BE.

It may be—there's no knowing—
That then, when buds are blowing,
When birds are greeting, greeting,
And all things mating, meeting,
   We two may come together,
   And find our springtime weather.

CIRCE.

You hold my heart in your slender hands,
In your cold, your cruel, careless hands.
In your beautiful hands, fanned by a breath
Like the breath of the rose, it is dying its death;

In your beautiful hands with their glitter of rings,
Each ring a trophy that scornfully sings
Of other hearts that have lain like mine
On your cruelly beautiful, pitiless shrine;

Of other hearts 'that have gone to their death,
Swooned to sleep by that sweet, sweet breath,

That breath of the rose that comes and goes
As the smiling, beautiful lips unclose,

When night after night down dizzying dances
They follow and follow your dazzling glances,
While round and round by the music whirled,
As I'd follow and follow you over the world!

Then hold me fast in your slender hands,
In your cruelly beautiful, pitiless hands;
Let me forever be dying my death,
Swooned to sleep by that sweet, sweet breath.

Let me forever be whirling there,
Lost in a trance divinely fair;
Let me forever be stricken and slain,
And dying with this delicious pain!

MY LADY.

Here she comes, — my lady, — so fair and so fine
From the gold of her hair to the glitter and shine
Of her Pompadour silk with its ruffles of lace, —
A wonderful vision of fashion and grace.

Here she comes, — my lady, — drawing on the
    pink gloves
Which I know, even here, have the scent that
    she loves;
And soft, as she moves her fingers of snow,
I catch in the movement the sparkle and glow

Of the ring that I gave her, — the diamond
    solitaire
That marks her "my lady," in Vanity Fair;
My lady, — my jewel, — to have and to hold
As her diamond is held, — *in a setting of gold.*

My lady, — my jewel, — would she sparkle and
    glow
If into the light I should suddenly go,
And stand where her beautiful eyes would discover,
In the flash of a moment, the eyes of her lover?

Would she turn to my glance as the diamond
    turns
To the light all its rays, till it blushes and burns?

Should I, standing thus, in that moment, — her
  lover, —
Be the light, all the light of her soul to discover?

Ah, my lady, — my jewel, — so fair and so fine,
Of your soul I have had little token or sign;
When I put on your finger that diamond solitaire,
I knew I was buying in Vanity Fair!

———

AND now I sit down daily with a face
As still as Death's, and keep an outward grace
Of silence, while the heart within, at Fate,
Clamors and frets behind its iron gate.

MISUNDERSTOOD.

They chide you for being so gay;
You have reckless spirits, they say,
And moods like an April day,
    Madeline.

Reckless and flippant and light,
I heard them call you last night,
When your mirth rose to its height,
    Madeline.

Reckless and flippant and light, —
I, who knew you aright,
Knew 't was a pitiful slight,
    Madeline.

For I knew what none of them guessed,
That, if your heart were at rest,
Your lips would be slower to jest,
    Madeline.

Then let them reprove as they may:
If it eases your heart to be gay,
To laugh ever so light, laugh away,
    Madeline, Madeline.

OUT OF THE WINDOW.[1]

OUT of the window she leaned, and laughed,
   A girl's laugh, idle and foolish and sweet, —
Foolish and idle, it dropped like a call,
   Into the crowded, noisy street.

Up he glanced at the glancing face,
   Who had caught the laugh as it fluttered and fell,
And eye to eye for a moment there
   They held each other as if by a spell.

All in a moment passing there, —
And into her idle, empty day,
All in that moment something new
Suddenly seemed to find its way.

And through and through the clamorous hours
That made his clamorous busy day,
A girl's laugh, idle and foolish and sweet,
Into every bargain found its way.

And through and through the crowd of the streets,
At every window in passing by,
He looked a moment, and seemed to see
A pair of eyes like the morning sky.

Cambridge : Printed by Welch, Bigelow, & Co.

www.ingramcontent.com/pod-product-compliance
Lightning Source LLC
Chambersburg PA
CBHW032136160426
43197CB00008B/661